Job's Choir

Essays From the Intersection of Grief and Hope

Charles Eugene Poole

© 2023
Published in the United States by Nurturing Faith Inc., Macon, GA,
www.goodfaithmedia.org

Library of Congress Cataloging-in-Publication Data is available.

ISBN: 978-1-63528-238-2

All rights reserved. Printed in the United States of America

To
Northminster Baptist Church
Jackson, Mississippi

Contents

Preface
vii

Introduction
ix

Why?
1

How?
9

Prayer and Pain
13

The Final Thin Place
19

Last Time Grief, First Time Grief
23

On Grieving the Loss of a Dream
27

On Making the Most of What's Left
30

When It's Time to Be Glad
37

First Bird
41

Job's Choir
44

Epilogue
49

Preface

Job's Choir is a grief book; a collection of essays from the corner where grief meets hope.

That it is a grief book helps explain why *Job's Choir* is such a brief book: Partly because to seek to speak of the tender wonders of grief and hope is soon to reach the limits of speech; and partly because there might be a moment someday when it would be helpful for us to have a grief book small enough to place in the hand of someone who is bearing a deep sorrow, facing a difficult change or grieving a lasting loss.

It is perhaps important to offer here an admittedly peripheral, but hopefully helpful, word about language for God in *Job's Choir*.

Because I am a person of faith writing from the perspective of faith, there are, in this small book, many times when the name of God appears, but there are no times when pronouns are used for God. The reason for that is this: Pronouns most often indicate gender—he, she, him, her. Gender is a human category, and God is God, not human. Therefore, I try never knowingly to use pronouns for God.

The Bible's usage of the male pronouns *he* and *him* for God should not be taken to mean that God is a man, any more than the frequency of the metaphor "Father" for God should be literalized to say the same. The predominant maleness of the Bible's images and metaphors for God is more a reflection of the patriarchal culture that prevailed at the time of the writing of scripture than an indication that God is a man.

Indeed, according to what we find in the Bible's first creation poem, in Genesis 1:26-27, if God had a pronoun, it might need to be "they": "Then God said, 'Let us create humankind in our image, according to our likeness' … So [God] created humankind in God's image...Male and female [God] created them." ...God, referring to God's self as "us," and creating humans in God's image as both male and female... God, in the spiritual poetry of the creation story, beyond binary, transcending gender, past pronouns.

Needless to say, many truly wonderful people use gender-specific pronouns for God. My purpose here is not to question their practice, but to explain mine.

I am deeply grateful to Bruce Gourley and Jackie Riley of Good Faith Media and Nurturing Faith. Without their help, neither *Job's Choir* nor *The Path to Depth* would yet have seen the light of day.

The dedication of *Job's Choir* is to Northminster Baptist Church in Jackson, Mississippi; a small gesture of enormous gratitude for a congregation of deep and dear souls to whom Marcia and I owe debts of love we can never repay.

I close these opening words with thanksgiving to, and for, our family:

Josh and Bett
Ansley, Emma Kate, Charlotte, Walker, and Ailey

Maria and James
Mary Hazel, Marcia, David, Brock, and Mason

… each and all, light and joy, to Marcia and me, and many more.
For which we say, "Thanks be to God."

Introduction

There is a long list of ways things can go wrong in this life. None of us will go through all of them, but all of us will go through some of them.

And when we do, when we find ourselves going through some crushing loss or hard struggle we did not get to go around, one name that often comes to mind, for many of us, is *Job*, whose ancient story, in the Bible book that bears his name, is largely about living into, through, and beyond the hardest and worst that life can bring.

Job's story is home to so much tragedy that, even beyond the Bible, Job's name is synonymous with suffering. In fact, Job's losses were so devastating, his grief so overwhelming, that, more than once, Job prayed to die.

In Job 3:20, he asked, "Why is light given to one in misery, and life to the bitter in soul, who long for death … who are glad when they find the grave?"

In Job 6:8-9, he prayed, "O that I might have my request, and that God would grant my desire; that it would please God to cut me off."

And, again, in Job 10:18-19, he cried, "If only I had died before any eye had seen me."

… A chorus of despair in which Job's is not the Bible's only voice. Take, for example:

- Moses, who is reported to have said to God, "If this is the way you are going to treat me, put me to death at once" (Num. 11:15).
- Elijah, who is reported to have prayed, "It is enough now, O LORD, take away my life" (1 Kgs. 19:4).
- Jonah, who is reported to have protested, "O LORD, please take my life from me, for it is better for me to die than to live" (Jonah 4:3).

Job's choir, I call them: Moses, Elijah, Jonah, and all the others, unnamed and unknown, beyond the Bible and across the centuries, who, like Job, were sure that they could not go on; souls so weary that they joined Job in that deepest prayer of deepest despair; "If you love me, let me die."

… A prayer that, as far as we know, was never answered in the Bible. Moses, Elijah, Jonah, and Job all prayed to die, and all of them woke up the next morning to face the same fears and fear the same faces, all over again. They may have believed that they could not go on, but they did.

Which is often so, as well, for us. Even in those moments when we are most certain that we cannot go on, we do. The question is almost never *"Will we go on?"* The question is almost always *How?* How do we go on when we are most certain that we cannot?

The simple words that are gathered in this small book are hopeful reflections on that quiet question: *"How do we go on when we cannot go on?"*—essays from the intersection of grief and hope.

If a book could hold a job, this one would be a street preacher; not the yelling-through-a-bullhorn kind, but a less loud kind of street preacher; the Quaker-quiet-crossing-guard-at-the-intersection-where-grief-meets-hope kind.

The noun "essay" that the subtitle assigns to the words that huddle here is an intentional choice, because of its close kinship to the old verb "assay," which, once upon a time, meant "to try."

Which is what the words huddled here are; *tries* at the truth, earnest efforts, certain to fail, because to seek to speak of such mysteries as grief and hope is, in the words of the late poet Byron Herbert Reese, to "Pledge our tongue to a speechless kingdom." "Each attempt," as T.S. Eliot once lamented, "a different kind of failure".

But, still, we try. We can't not. There is too much pain in the world, and in our lives, not, at least, to try. And so, with Job, we begin at *Why?*

Why?

"*Why?* is the question mark that is twisted like a fishhook in the heart." That piercing sentence from Nicholas Wolterstorff's *Lament for a Son* could just as easily have lived on the lips of Job, who, early in the book that bears his name, asked God, "Why have you made me your target?" (7:20)—Job's way of asking God why Job's life was turning out to be so difficult and painful, the kind of question in which many others have joined Job.

Take, for example, Jeremiah's unforgettable lament, "Why is my pain unceasing, and my wound incurable?" (Jer. 15:18).

And then there is Habakkuk, who asked God, "Why do you make me see wrongdoing and look at trouble?" (Hab. 1:3).

And the psalmist, calling from the depths of despair, "My God, my God, why have you forsaken me?" (Ps. 22:1), words that eventually found their anguished echo on the lips of Jesus who, from the cross, is reported to have said the same, "My God, my God, why …?" (Matt. 27:6).

Why? is the question mark that is twisted like a fishhook in many hearts—Job's choir, singing in baffled unison the disappointed demand of bewildered faith, *Why?*

In the religious world of my childhood, to ask God "Why?" was frowned upon as the kind of question that was assumed to be a sign of doubt about God. But the longer I live, the more I know that faith, not doubt, is where our *whys* begin. If we didn't have faith in God, we wouldn't expect anything from God, and if we didn't expect anything from God, we wouldn't wonder why God hasn't done more to spare us from the crushing sorrow or deliver us from the exhausting struggle.

If God cares, and if God can, then why doesn't God step in more often to spare, heal, shield, and protect?

That kind of question has been asked by so many for so long that, somewhere along the way, it was given a special name: *theodicy*.

Theodicy is a four-syllable word for *Why?* If God is all-loving and all-powerful, then why is there so much suffering and pain, evil and violence, tragedy and trouble in the world? If God cares, and if God can, then why doesn't God step in more often and stop the worst before it happens?

(Of course, here it may be important to say that none of us can ever know all from which we have been spared. Since the things from which we have been protected didn't happen, we don't know what they are.)

In a well-intentioned effort to help make sense of life, the church has sometimes sought to say *why* for those who ask *why*—to offer answers to the theodicy question—answers that sometimes sound not unlike the answers Job's friends gave Job when Job asked *Why?*

As you may remember, in the days following the tragedies that came to Job's life, Job's friends—Elipaz, Bildad, and Zophar—came to visit Job in his grief. At first, they were content to sit with Job in silence. Job 2:13 says, "They sat with Job on the ground seven days and seven nights, and no one spoke a word to him, for they saw that his suffering was very great."

Though it would soon splinter into too much talking and too many words, their initial showing up in solidarity and sitting near in silence is, for us all, a beautiful example of one helpful way to be present with those who are struggling, frightened, and sad … the quiet act of simply showing up.

There is, as the writer of Ecclesiastes once famously said, a time for words and a time for silence; helpful wisdom for all of us in those moments when we are reluctant to go to someone in great pain or deep sorrow because "we don't know what to say." Sometimes it is enough just to show up. Sometimes it is *best* just to show up.

William Sloane Coffin, in his remarkable sermon, "Alex' Death," said that sometimes we say too much in the face of crushing grief in an effort to "pretty-up a situation the bleakness of which we simply cannot face." Coffin says that what those who are hurting most often need, instead of so much talking, are friends who are "content to hold your hand, not to quote anybody or say anything; people who simply bring flowers or food—the basics of beauty and life—and who sign letters, *Your broken-hearted sister.*"

In his beautiful book, *Let Your Life Speak*, Parker Palmer says something similar: "One of the hardest things we must do sometimes is to be present to another person's pain without trying to fix it; to simply stand respectfully at the edge of that person's mystery and misery."

Which is what Job's friends did, *at first*. Elipaz, Bildad, and Zophar were, at first, content to sit in silence at the edge of Job's mystery and misery. But, like many of us, they soon felt the well-intentioned need to say something, to try and make some sense of the crushing sorrow that had come to Job's life; a need to explain that many of us understand and share. In the face of the hardest and worst tragedies and losses, many of us genuinely long for some sure and certain answer to the *Why?* that is twisted like a fishhook in the heart.

For Elipaz, Bildad, and Zophar, the explanation for Job's sorrow lay in Job's life. Job's trouble must be punishment for sin: "Think now, who that was innocent ever perished?... Those who plow iniquity and sow trouble reap the same" (Job 4:7a-8), said Elipaz.

With those words, Elipaz offered Job a "cause-and-effect" way of looking at life that appears in several places in the Bible, particularly in that ancient editorial stream that much of the best scholarship we have refers to as the Deuteronomist.

The Deuteronomist's theology might best be described as an "if-then" understanding of the way life works: *if* we obey God, *then* God will protect and bless us; but *if* we disobey God, *then* God will punish and curse us.... A way of understanding life that is captured in:

- Deuteronomy 5:33, "You must follow exactly the path that the LORD your God has commanded you, so that ... it may go well with you."
- Deuteronomy 8:19, "If you forget the LORD your God...I solemnly warn that you shall surely perish."
- Deuteronomy 11:26-28, "See, I am setting before you today a blessing and a curse; the blessing, if you obey the commandments of the LORD your God...and the curse, if you do not obey the commandments of the LORD your God."

This sort of if-then, cause-and-effect way of looking at life, which found an early advocate in the Deuteronomist, finds an eloquent echo in Elipaz, when Elipaz says to Job, "Think now, who that was innocent ever perished? ... As I have seen, those who plow iniquity and sow trouble reap the same." Or, as the Deuteronomist says, "Do right and be blessed; do wrong and be cursed"; a way of thinking in which all of life's joys and sorrows are seen as a series of transactions between God and us: We please God, God gives us protection. We displease God, God sends us suffering.

The attraction that this way of looking at life has long held for so many is not difficult to understand. It can, after all, help make life make sense. As the Irish poet Padraig Ó Tuama has wisely observed, we humans are "pattern-seeking, meaning-making creatures," wherein may lie the lure of the transactional theology of the Deuteronomist.

As the phrase would suggest, *transactional theology* sees our life with God as a series of *transactions*.

One familiar example of transactional theology would be the widely held view of the atonement that teaches that Jesus died on the cross to pay the price that God required before God could be reconciled to humanity— the crucifixion as a transaction between Jesus and God.

Another example of transactional theology would be the view of prayer that says that if we don't receive the help or healing for which we prayed, it must be because we didn't pray hard enough for long enough, or with sufficient faith or enough prayer partners. If only we had given God more of what God wanted (faith, persistence, belief, prayer partners), God would have given us more of what we wanted (healing, rescue, deliverance, success). Prayer as transaction: If we give God what God demands, then God will give us what we desire.

All of which leaves us with a very human God; a God we have created in our image; a kind of God who reacts and responds in familiar, predictable, human, *transactional* ways.

The Deuteronomist's reward-and-punishment transactional theology can be very comforting in its logical predictability—until it breaks down. Which, apparently, is a central point of the book of Job.

In Robert Frost's play about the book of Job, *A Masque of Reason*, there is that moment when God, who is apologizing to Job for all the trouble Job endured, thanks Job for helping God to "stultify the Deuteronomist"—the book of Job, posing the ultimate biblical challenge to the pattern-seeking, meaning-making, cause-and-effect, transactional theology of the Deuteronomist.

The "stultification of the Deuteronomist" is woven into the complex fabric of Job's tragic story in the opening verse of the Bible book that bears Job's name, where Job is established as the ultimate example of genuine righteousness:

"There once was a man in the land of Uz whose name was Job. That man was blameless and upright, one who feared God and turned away from evil" (Job 1:1), an assessment that will be reiterated in Job 1:8, where God asks Satan, "Have you noticed my servant Job? There is no one like him on the earth; a blameless and upright man who fears God and turns away from evil," and in Job 2:3, where God again praises Job as the most righteous person on the entire planet.

Thus, once Job's wonderful world comes crashing down around him, tragedy upon tragedy, loss upon loss, (Job 1:13-19, 2:7-8) we already know that Job's troubles are not punishments for some hidden fault or failure. The writer of the book of Job has gone to great lengths to be sure that we know that Job's story will not conform to the Deuteronomist's cause-and-effect, reward-and-punishment explanation of human suffering.

All of which puts a biblical frame around an undeniable truth that most of us have already observed just by living our ordinary, everyday lives: The dearest people we have ever known sometimes bear the heaviest burdens we have ever seen.

"Job's choir," I call them; all those dear and good souls who, like Job, get up every morning and live lives of integrity and generosity, kindness and truth, and, yet, like Job, suffer sorrows that bend them low with loss and pain, disappointment and grief; the transactional theology of the Deuteronomist "stultified," not only by Job's ancient story, but, also, by countless souls since; beautiful souls living painful lives; their sorrows, like Job's, not attributable to any fault of their own.

Which is not to suggest that there is never any connection between choices and pain. To the contrary, the consequences of our choices often become the circumstances of our lives.

But, not always. As the popular colloquialism wisely declares, "Two things can be true." It is true that our choices matter, *and* that suffering is not always a consequence of something, just as success is not always a reward for something. As Jesus is reported to have said, the rain falls and the sun shines on the good and the bad, without regard for whether they are good or bad (Matt. 5:45).

All of which gives us no simple and settled answer to the theodicy question; which leaves us, still, to wonder, "Why?"

The answer to the theodicy question is beyond us. For many of us *Why?* will be, for as long as we live, the question mark twisted like a fishhook in our heart.

But, as Fred Buechner once wisely observed, concerning Job's *whys* and ours, even if Job had gotten the answers to all his questions, Job still would have been staring at ten empty chairs every morning and scratching at a thousand stinging sores every night. What Job *wanted* may have been the answers to resolve his questions, but what Job *needed* was the courage to live his life.

And the same is so for us all. There is nothing wrong or wasteful about asking *Why?* Indeed, for many of us, there are moments when we can't not ask *Why?* But, at some point, *Why?* will need to make room for *How?* on the mourners' bench.

How? … not instead of, but in addition to *Why?*

How? … as in "How do we go through what we did not get to go around?"

I want to ask you, as clearly as I can, to bear, with patience, all that is unresolved in your heart, and to try to love the questions themselves…Live the questions now. Perhaps then, someday, you will gradually, without noticing, live into the answer.

- Rainer Maria Rilke

How?

When life's next question is, "How will we go through what we did not get to go around?" one important answer is: "Not alone, but with the help of friends"; carried and held by the courage we draw from, and the strength we find in, what Stanley Hauerwas once called "a community capable of absorbing our grief."

Though I, myself, am an introvert (with hermit-leanings), even I have learned, across a lifetime of joy and sorrow, that burdens are best borne, not alone, but together.

In her remarkable poem "Heavy," the late Mary Oliver captured, with these tender words, how much we need others to help us carry our grief:

> That time
> I thought I could not
> go any closer to grief
> without dying
>
> I went closer,
> And I did not die.
> Surely God
> had [a] hand in this,
> As well as friends…

… The Spirit of God and the people of God, carrying us through things so hard that if someone had told us ahead of time we were going to have to go through them, we would have sworn we could never make it. But we do. We do go through. And as Mary Oliver said, "Surely [God] has a hand in that, as well as friends."

Some find those courage-friends in their book group or exercise group, at their workplace or coffee shop, in their building or on their street.

For many of us, the friends from whom we draw strength and in whom we find courage are those with whom we worship. For some, it happens at the synagogue, the temple, or the mosque. For others, myself among them, it happens in church.

Many years ago, in a sermon by the late minister and writer Welton Gaddy, I stumbled across a conversation between Carlyle Marney and his father, in which the elder Marney, now in the later years of his life, was lamenting to his famous preacher-son the lifelong fragility of his faith, to which the younger Marney, genuinely surprised, said, "Dad, I never knew. You always seem so strong. If you have lived so long with so much struggle and doubt, what has kept you going?" To which Mr. Marney replied, "I would always be alright if I could just make it to the meeting."

That has been the story of my life. I cannot speak for anyone else, but, as for me, *I would always be alright if I could just make it to the meeting.*

I know as well as anyone the blind spots and limits of the church. As Barbara Brown Taylor has wisely observed, "The work of God gets done in the world both because of, and in spite of, the church." But, however much growing in grace the church may yet need to do, the church is, for many, myself among them, the place where we find the most courage and strength, comfort and hope.

Sometimes it is a sermon or a song, a reading or a prayer, which gives us enough comfort and courage to face the week that waits. But mostly it is the people; the kindness and courage of the people of

God embodying for us the spirit of God, an alchemy of empathy and solidarity that creates the beautiful mystery of "a community capable of absorbing our grief."

It can happen any place "where two or three are gathered," as the scripture says. But, for many of us, it happens nowhere more so than in a congregation gathered in a spirit of love and prayer, kindness and care.

To return to where we started, when the question is *Why?*—as in "Why are we suffering?"—one answer is: "There is a long list of ways things can go wrong in this life. While none of us will go through all of them, all of us will go through some of them, not because God is that way but because life is that way."

Then, when the next question after *Why?* is *How*—as in "How do we go on when we cannot go on?"—one answer is: "With the courage we find in, and the strength we draw from, those with whom we share a caring community."

And, another answer, in the next chapter, to the "How do we go on?" question is "Through the strength we find in the life of prayer."

*It's not the weight you carry
but how you carry it—
books, bricks, grief—
it's all in the way
you embrace it, balance it, carry it
when you cannot, and would not,
put it down.*

-Mary Oliver

Prayer and Pain

Tucked away in a quiet corner of Marilynne Robinson's novel *Lila*, there is that memorable moment when Lila wonders what the difference is between praying and worrying.

Praying and worrying: sometimes it can be hard to tell where one ends and the other begins.

Which might also be said of praying and hoping, praying and dreaming, praying and wishing, praying and walking, praying and waiting, even praying and breathing. Where, even, does breathing end and praying begin? As Barbara Brown Taylor once wrote, "To say 'I love God but I don't pray much' would be like saying 'I love life but I don't breathe much'."

There once was a time when I thought Paul's admonition for us to "pray without ceasing" was impossible to do. But the longer I live, the more I find "praying without ceasing" impossible *not* to do. To live is to pray. To pray is to live. And, slowly, slowly, little by little, the more prayer becomes our life, the more our life becomes a prayer.

This is what the Quaker thinker Thomas Kelly called "life lived on two levels." In *A Testament of Devotion*, Kelly spoke of going through the day living life on two levels—not alternately, but simultaneously—on one level, working, playing, paying bills, preparing meals, attending meetings, living into the opportunities and obligations of an ordinary day, while, simultaneously, on a deeper level, listening for, and talking to, God; our attention, not divided and partial, but centered and deepened.

Prayer, as inevitable as breathing … Prayer, slowly becoming our life, until our life eventually becomes a prayer.

For many of us, there are seasons in life when much of our praying becomes something more like pleading. In times of deep pain, crushing loss or immobilizing fear, it is not only, as Lila said, hard to tell the difference between praying and worrying. It is also hard to discern praying from pleading; pleading with God to do for us that which we cannot do for ourselves.

It is in those pleading seasons of life when many of us are drawn to the transactional way of thinking about prayer; thinking of prayer as a transaction that does or does not "work" based on how much faith we have or how persistently we pray or how many prayer partners we recruit.

"If we pray hard enough, often enough, we can persuade God to place an impenetrable hedge of protection around us and those we love." That is the transactional view of prayer: If we give God what God demands, God will give us what we desire.

Many dear and good souls have long seen prayer that way, myself among them for the first half of my life. (And, in life's hardest moments, my "crisis theology" can take me back to it now). But, somewhere along the way, I came to see prayer, not as a transaction between us and God, but, rather, as our intimate and unceasing life with God. We plead for the relief or healing or help we need, not to keep our side of a bargain so God will be obligated to keep God's side, but because we can't not pour out our grief and our hope to God.

As C.S. Lewis' words are portrayed in the movie *Shadowlands*, "I don't pray to change God's mind. I pray because I can't not pray. My prayers pour forth by day and by night; waking and sleeping." ... A prayerful helplessness and a helpless prayerfulness that calls to mind, for me, that tender confession of Joanna Macy's, concerning her own spiritual journey: "I was a failure as an atheist ... because I could not cure myself of praying to a God I no longer believed in."

… Prayer, not as our transaction with God, but as our life with God. Waking and sleeping, working and playing, walking and resting, weeping and laughing, in joy and in sorrow, by day and by night, we pray without ceasing because we can't not.

Anne Lamott once wisely wrote that there are really only two kinds of prayers: "Help me, Help me, Help me" and "Thank you, Thank you, Thank you," words that, for many of us, ring especially true in life's most frightening and sorrowful seasons.

In life's most crushing moments, our prayers become as raw as Jesus' cry from the cross, "My God, my God, why have you forsaken me?" and Jeremiah's anguished lament, "Why is my pain unceasing and my wound incurable?" As Mary Oliver said in one of her poems, "I know a lot of fancy words. I tear them from my mouth, and then I pray."

In my own life with God, that sometimes takes the shape of a single simple sentence: "God, if you can do *that*, you can do *this*."

I will see a sunrise or sunset, rainbow or robin, redbird or rose, and say to God: "God, if you can do that, you can do this. If you can draw that pink and purple sunrise sky, you can cure this disease. If you can paint that pastel rainbow, you can lift this deep despair. If you can do *that* up there in the air, you can do *this* down here on the ground."

I am speaking of these things with very simple words; words that, needless to say, do not begin to capture the wonder and mystery of prayer. As Paul said to the Romans, "We do not know how to pray." Indeed. Careful speech requires us to say that to seek to speak of the wonder and mystery of prayer is to "pledge our tongues to a speechless kingdom," as Byron Herbert Reese so beautifully put it. Each attempt, "a raid on the inarticulate, with shabby equipment, certain to fail," as T.S. Eliot said concerning all such efforts at all such mysteries.

As life moves on, we all find, and adjust, our own ways of speaking of prayer. Many of the dearest and best people I know speak of prayer in ways I once did, but no longer do; in that transactional way that speaks of prayer as "working" or "being answered," some genuine and sincere souls referring to everything from profitable business deals to timely home sales as "answers to prayer" and "God-things."

As someone who lives in a well-nigh perpetual conversation with God about well-nigh everything one can name, I understand that way of speaking of prayer, but I do not share it. I believe that before God got that involved in stock sales and real estate listings, God would heal all the patients and empty all the beds at St. Jude's and M.D. Anderson.

Of all the words I have read about prayer, the ones that ring most true to me travel in Barbara Brown Taylor's book *An Altar in the World*, in which Reverend Taylor tells the story of a friend who was praying for God to intervene and save a loved one who was dying. As the person pleaded with God to step in and do something miraculous, he turned to Barbara Brown Taylor and asked,

> You want to know whether I really believe God will intervene like that? Honestly, I don't think it through, not now. I tell God what I want. I'm not smart enough or strong enough to do anything else, and besides, there's no time. So I tell God what I want and trust God to sort it out.

When it comes to prayer, that is the story of my life. I just tell God the truth about what I want and need, and trust God with the rest. I'm not smart enough or strong enough to do anything else.

Across many years of living that way, I have seen moments when prayer changed our circumstances, and I have seen moments when our circumstances changed our prayers. But, either way, still, we pray, even when that means adjusting the arc of our prayers to more nearly match the trajectory of our lives.

The remarkable singer/songwriter Iris Dement has a deeply spiritual song about the death of a child. The title of the song is, "The Night I Learned How Not to Pray," a resignation I understand, but a place I have not yet gone. I just keep praying for the next best thing, bending the arc of my prayers to match the trajectory of my life.

As long as there is something else to want, there is something more to pray.

As John Claypool used to say, it is good for us to open our arms wide when we pray, because if we cup our hands too tightly, refusing to accept any gift but the one we want most, we may miss the other gifts God is going to give. Better to open our arms all the way out and spread our hands wide enough to catch whatever gift God gives.

The gift God gives may be the miracle we want. But if the gift God gives isn't the miracle we want— protection, healing, safety, and success—it will be the miracle we need—courage, comfort, and strength enough to see us through the wonderful thing God might have done but did not do.

Though we may not receive the first best gift for which we prayed, we wouldn't want to miss the next best gift. So, we pray with our arms and hands, hearts and minds wide open; open wide enough to receive whatever gift God sends our way.

… Praying without ceasing, not because we should, but because we can't not; no longer able to tell the difference between praying and worrying, praying and walking, praying and hoping or dreaming or breathing or living.

… Prayer, slowly becoming our life until our life eventually becomes a prayer.

Faith is what you have left when you don't get the miracle.

-Barbara Brown Taylor

The Final Thin Place

But even prayer, wonderful as it is, cannot forever delay death. Even Lazarus, who Jesus raised from death, had to die again.

The same is so, as far as we know, for the others Jesus is reported to have raised from death. The twelve-year-old daughter of Jairus and the son of the widow of Nain, like Lazarus, got to live again, but both had to die again.

For many of us, it is hard to know how to speak of death. Not knowing how best to speak of the mystery of that moment, I most often find myself speaking of death as "entering the nearer presence of God" or "crossing over to the Other Side," phrases that, though different from one another, say essentially the same:

To die is to cross over to the Other Side, into the nearer presence of God. … A passing from this life to the next that I sometimes think of as "the final thin place."

The precise origins of the phrase "thin place" are largely lost to the mist of history, but Celtic spirituality seems to be the source from which that beautiful description of sacred nearness first emerged; thin places being those moments, spaces, experiences, and places when the veil that separates this side from the Other Side becomes so thin that we could almost step right through.

For those who have eyes to see, life is thick with thin places. As Elizabeth Barrett Browning so lyrically put it,

> Earth's crammed with heaven,
> And every common bush afire with God.
> But only [those] who see
> Take off [their] shoes.

Browning's verse is an obvious allusion to the story of the burning bush in Exodus 3, where Moses is reported to have removed his shoes as a gesture of reverence as he watched an ordinary bush burn with the presence of God. ... Moses, finding himself in a thin place; one of those moments in life when the curtain that separates this world from the next grows so thin that it seems you could almost step right through.

And then, one day, we do. One day we do step right through, into the nearer presence of God, over on the Other Side—death, life's final thin place.

For some, death comes as an enemy to be resisted. For others, death comes as a friend to be welcomed; for some, a tragic shock; for others, a tender relief.

We need to learn, in church, synagogue, temple, and mosque, that death is not always a battle lost. The same is important for physicians and nurses to know, as well as assisted living caregivers and hospice workers.

While most people get to live until they have to die, some people have to live until they get to die... Death coming, for some, as a tragic shock, but, for others, as a tender relief.

In either case, death is life's final thin place. When death comes as naturally and peacefully as a last breath here and a first breath there, and when death comes as an unspeakable shock and an unbearable loss, death is life's final thin place; the veil between this life and the next thinning away. Just as there was an effacing at our coming into the world, there is an effacing at our going from the world—life, thinning out into death.

… Death, the final thin place, not only at the moment of death, but always and ever; time and distance collapsing into a different kind of connection between life on this side and life on the Other Side … Those who have died, ever absent from us in sight, sound, and touch, and ever present with us in memory, story, and spirit.

… Death; the final, and eternal, thin place. Those who yet live, held in God's hands, and those who have died, held in God's hands … The same hands that are holding them there, holding us here … All of us, living and dead, here and there, held, together, in the same hands; the hands that will hold us, and never let us go.

… Time and distance, collapsing into an eternal thin place on that eventual, inevitable someday that, for all of us, will be the last day.

Funeral

Gathered again
Astride the mending seam
Where the weaving hands
Of life and death
Stitch time to eternity
And eternity to time.
Our hearts and minds
Full and tender
With memories and stories,
Grief and relief.

- CEP

Last Time Grief, First Time Grief

Before we get to the last day of our life, there will be, for most of us, many last times in our life—one last day, many last times.

Concerning the tenderness of last times, Mary Connell wrote a remarkable poem, "Final Sightings," in which, after naming some of the many things that will happen in our lives for the last time, she summed it all up with this:

> And so it is with any sweet occurrence
> That lends any sense or comfort to our lives;
> The ultimate gaze and the final phrase
> Are pretty hard to recognize.
> It will happen for the last time
> And very likely no one will know
> When it happened that it stopped happening.

I stumbled across those words when I was young, in my twenties. And, somehow, they found their way to someplace near the center of my soul, where they have made, for me, a small, quiet, deeply sacred difference.

I learned, from this simple poem, to pay attention in a different kind of way; to live with an eye out for last times—what Fred Buechner called "paying attention to our life."

To be mindful that everything will happen for the last time is to live more deeply into each time.

Once I learned to live that way, I began to have moments when I wondered which time would be the last time. For example, I remember wondering, many years ago, "Is this the last time I will be able to carry Josh or Maria up the stairs?"

At Thanksgiving and Christmas gatherings, I have long looked around the table and wondered if this time will be the last time we will all be together.

Years ago, I started picking up particularly colorful autumn leaves while walking. Having practiced paying attention in that way for so long, I am now afraid that if I stop noticing them, I might stop seeing them. Often when I stop to lift a leaf and study briefly its beauty, the Spirit reminds me that there will be a last time when I will be able to bend to lift a leaf; a last time, even, when I will be able to go on sunrise prayer walks.

Of course, we usually do not know when something is happening for the last time. As the poem says, "It will happen for the last time, and very likely no one will know when it happened that it stopped happening." But, to the extent that we are able to recognize the last times, they often bring with them a quiet, tender sadness; a particular kind of sadness that might best be called "last time grief," a last time grief that soon becomes first time grief.

Because the next time after the last time is the first time, last time grief soon becomes first time grief.

We may not always know which time is the last, but we always know which time is the first: the first Thanksgiving or Christmas or birthday or anniversary after the death or the divorce, the retirement or the relocation, the tragedy or the diagnosis, the heartbreak or the change.

And first times, like last times, can bring their own quiet tenderness; the kind of sadness that is beautifully described in John Koenig's book, *The Dictionary of Obscure Sorrows*, in which Koenig traces the roots of our word *sadness* to the Latin word for *fullness*, sadness and fullness both rising from the same source.

… Last time grief and first time grief, each a sadness that is a version of fullness; our hearts and minds full and tender with the awareness that life is changing and with the longing for what once was and no longer is.

… Last time grief and first time grief, each a quiet sadness and a tender fullness; one coming so soon after the other that it can sometimes be hard to tell where one ends and the other begins.

… All the more reason to stay awake to the passing, fragile nature of life and to live each day as though someday will be the last day.

I can't look at everything hard enough.

-Act III of Thornton Wilder's *Our Town*

On Grieving the Loss of a Dream

The death of the long-held hope of a deep, dear dream is another kind of loss, which brings its own kind of grief.

Whenever I think about how hard it can be to grieve the death of a dream, I tend to wander away to Pisgah, that mountain in Deuteronomy 34, where God is reported to have given Moses a glimpse of the Promised Land; Moses, finally able to lay eyes on it, but never able to set foot on it.

Moses was so close—near enough to see the dream come true. But, though he finally got to see it, he never got to have it.

Which happens a lot in life; many of us, not unlike Moses on Pisgah, having to learn when and how to give a dream a decent burial.

If the late Wayne Oates was right when he said that "Grief is the aftermath of any deeply felt loss," then the death of a dream is definitely on the more quietly complex end of the list of losses that leave us grieving—Job's choir, saving a section for those who are occasionally haunted by the what-if ghost of something almost.

As John Greenleaf Whittier wrote, all those years ago, "Of all sad words of tongue or pen, the saddest are these, 'It might have been'."

… Words that sound a lot like a eulogy for a dream, which doesn't happen often—at least, not out loud.

We don't usually send flowers or deliver casseroles when dreams die. Most of the time, no one but the dreamer knows to place their hand over their heart. There might be an occasional obituary for a dream tucked away somewhere in a prayer journal or diary, but none that any of us have ever seen in the Sunday paper.

But, if they ever do start holding funerals for dreams, we'll all be wearing black every day, meeting to pay our last respects to another one that got away.

In the meantime, until they do start placing headstones on dream graves, we might all practice, more and more intentionally, the spiritual discipline of kind and careful speech: what Mary Oliver called "walking slowly and bowing often," the kind of life I call "Quaker quiet." … Living and speaking so thoughtfully and mindfully that our presence and words will be healing and gentle, even when we are not aware that they need to be.

Because one never knows when, in what appears to be an ordinary moment or conversation, we might unknowingly be stepping on a grave.

… For a dream.

Neiman Marcus Girl, Walmart World

Her dreams were always wider
Than her hometown could provide her.
She's a Times Square girl,
Living in a town square world.

She does her best to hide her,
But you can see it deep inside her.
She's a Neiman Marcus girl,
Living in a Walmart world.

Watching the going geese fly
As far as she can see;
Aching to be the W
That follows their leaving V.

It was hard to stop believing
That someday she'd be leaving,
For a going places girl,
In a staying here world.

The dream that never got given a whirl,
The sand that never quite turned to pearl,
For a living the dream girl,
In a dreaming the life world.

-CEP

On Making the Most of What's Left

Or, as Wendell Berry once wisely wrote, "We live the given life, not the planned."

The life we have may not be the life we planned, but, as far as we know, the life we have is our one and only turn at life in this world—what Mary Oliver called our "one wild and precious life."

And, someday it will end. For all of us, someday is going to be the last day. And, while no one can say for certain, as far as we know, we are not going to get to come back around, do this over, and get it right the next time. The life we have been given may not be the life we dreamed, wanted, imagined, or planned, but, as far as we know, it is the only one we are ever going to have. So, how will we make the most of whatever is left of it?

That question has rarely been raised more memorably than in the Hebrew Bible book of Jeremiah. Most of the best scholarship we have believes that the book of Jeremiah, like much of the First Testament, was formed by that long displacement of the people of Judah that is known, within and beyond the Bible, as "the exile"—the forced relocation to Babylon of many of the people of the southern kingdom of Israel (Judah); a season of captivity that lasted roughly sixty years, from about 597 BCE, when the Babylonian army carried away a portion of the people of Judah, until about 539 BCE, when Cyrus, ruler of Persia, conquered Babylon and set the captives free.

According to the book of Jeremiah, among the people of Judah who were left behind in Jerusalem during the exile was the one we know as Jeremiah, author of the Bible book that bears his name.

Among the most well-known "exile passages" in all of scripture is a piece of correspondence between Jeremiah and the people of Judah who had been carried away captive to live in exile in Babylon: a letter that appears to have been prompted by some preachers who were predicting that the exile would soon be coming to an end; one, named Hananiah, declaring that the exile would last only two years (Jer. 28:1-10).

Jeremiah's answer to the optimistic promises of a brief exile and a soon return was a word of clear-eyed, albeit unwelcome, realism. In one of the most beloved and familiar passages in all the First Testament, Jeremiah is reported to have said to the people of Judah in exile in Babylon:

> Thus says the Lord of hosts, the God of Israel: "Do not let the prophets and the diviners who are among you deceive you ... for it is a lie that they are prophesying to you in my name ... Only when Babylon's seventy years are completed will I visit you, and I will fulfill to you my promise and bring you back to this place." (Jer. 29:8-10)

Seventy years, says Jeremiah. The exile is going to last, not *two* years, as the popular, positive, sunny-side-of-the-street preachers had promised, but *seventy* years, which Psalm 90:10 names as a person's normal life expectancy.

In other words, what Jeremiah was telling the people of God in exile was that they were there for the rest of their lives. Anyone old enough to hear and understand the message was probably in exile to stay.

"This is it," said Jeremiah. "This life in exile may not be the life you dreamed, planned, or imagined, but it is the life you have been given. If you put your life on hold until after the exile is over, then you will go to your grave with whatever was left of the only life you are ever going to have, on hold."

Jeremiah's advice to the exiled people of God was that they should stop waiting for life to get back to normal, and begin living whatever was left of their life as deeply, fully, and faithfully as they could:

> Thus says the Lord of hosts, the God of Israel, to all the exiles…
> "Build houses and live in them, plant gardens and eat what they produce … multiply there, and do not decrease." (Jer. 29:4-6)

Don't let your longing for the life you cannot have in Jerusalem keep you from living the life you can have in Babylon, said Jeremiah. *It may not be the life you wanted, dreamed, imagined, or planned, but it is the life you have. So, build a house and live in it. Plant a garden and eat from it. Because this is it. If you put your life on hold until it goes back to normal, you will go to your grave with your life on hold. Don't sacrifice the only life you can have on the altar of the longed-for life you can't have.*

Jeremiah's sermon to the exiles is not unlike another sermon, preached centuries later by Harry Emerson Fosdick at the Riverside Church in New York City. The title of Fosdick's famous sermon was "Handling Life's Second Best," and, like Jeremiah's sermon to the exiles, it was all about the spiritual discipline of adjusting—what Wendell Berry called living "the given life, not the planned." The point of Fosdick's message was that very few people get to live the life they planned, dreamed, or imagined. Most of us face changes, challenges, and disappointments to which we must adjust and with which we must live.

In their beautiful volume *Pilgrim Souls*, Elizabeth Powers and Amy Mandecker say, concerning Emily Dickinson, that, at some point,

"Her soul reached a settlement with her life" … what Fosdick called "learning how to handle life's second best" … echoes of Jeremiah's admonition to the exiles to come to terms with the life they had and live it as deeply, fully, and faithfully as they could … making the most of whatever was left of their lives.

All of which is helpful for any of us for whom life has taken hard turns, which is most of us. Everyone is always adjusting to something.

We live the given life, not the planned; our soul, at some point, having to reach a settlement with our life; all of us, at some point in our lives "going into exile," most of us more than once, our lives disrupted and changed in ways we never dreamed or imagined would be ours to face and endure.

And what then? As the Scottish preacher A.J. Gossip famously posed the question, "When life tumbles in, what then?" When we are living through our own exile seasons, separated, like Jeremiah's exiles, from the life we want and can't have by the life we have and can't change, what then?

Perhaps one small first step is to name, with specific word care, the things we can change and the things we cannot change.

There are always parts of our lives that we can choose to change. If we are unkind and hurtful; reckless and mean; racist, homophobic and xenophobic; materialistic, greedy, and selfish, there is something we can do about that. We can choose to change, and then prayerfully practice becoming new—what scripture calls "repentance."

In the words of Mary Oliver, we can "wake each morning with thirst for the goodness we do not have." It may take much prayer and practice, and it may not happen all at once or once and for all, but there are some parts of our lives that, with the help of the Spirit of God and the people of God, can be changed.

But there are other parts of our lives that cannot be changed. Like the recipients of Jeremiah's letter to those who were in exile in Babylon, we sometimes have to come to terms with irreversible losses and irrevocable changes.

The best we can do in the face of what cannot be changed is to decide to live whatever is left of the one and only life we are ever going to have as deeply, fully, and faithfully as we can—what Jeremiah called "building a house and planting a garden"—not once things "get back to normal," which is never going to happen, but now, in exile.

And Jeremiah did not stop there. After Jeremiah counseled the people of Judah to live whatever was left of their lives as deeply, fully, and faithfully as possible, he called them further: to live their lives in exile, not only deeply, fully, and faithfully, but also bravely, beautifully, and gracefully.

"Pray for those who carried you away captive into exile," said Jeremiah, in one of the more expansive and inclusive moments in all of scripture:

> Thus says the LORD of hosts, the God of Israel, to all the exiles… "Seek the welfare of the city where I have sent you into exile, and pray to the LORD on its behalf, for in its welfare you will find your welfare." (Jer. 29:4, 7)

With those words, Jeremiah called the grieving people of God in exile to become the growing people of God in exile, not only to endure and survive, but to grow and thrive;

…to see themselves bound, even to their Babylonian captors, in what Martin Luther King Jr. so memorably called "a web of mutuality,"

... to pray and work for the welfare even of their enemies, because, in the family of God, which is the whole human family, everyone's welfare is inextricably bound up with everyone else's welfare.

Jeremiah's invitation to the grieving exiles, not only to live whatever was left of their lives deeply, fully, and faithfully, but also beautifully, bravely, and gracefully, calls to mind for me that memorable passage in *An Altar in the World* in which Barbara Brown Taylor wrote,

> I have seen pain twist people and those who love them into exhausted rags with all the hope squeezed out of them. I have also seen people in whom pain seems to have burned away everything extra, everything trivial, everything petty and less than noble, until they have become see-through with light.

And, perhaps, sometimes, it is not one or the other, but both in the same suffering soul; an exhausted rag, luminous with love; squeezed-out by pain *and* see-through with light. Because everything but love has been burned away; nothing but love has managed to stay ... pain, as surgical as surgery is painful.

For many weary souls, living through, and with, disruptions and disappointments, sorrow and loss, there sometimes comes a day when we discover that, while we were slowly, prayerfully working to make the best of the worst, the worst was deeply, quietly working to make the best of us.

Before you know kindness as the deepest thing inside,
*   you must know sorrow as the other deepest thing.*
You must wake up with sorrow.
You must speak to it till your voice
*   catches the thread of all sorrows*
*   and you see the size of the cloth.*
Then it is only kindness that makes sense anymore,
*   only kindness that ties your shoes,*
*   and sends you out into the day…*

-Naomi Shihab Nye

When It's Time to Be Glad

"Here is the world. Beautiful and terrible things will happen," Fred Buechner once wrote.

Which calls to mind Mrs. Soames in Act III of Thornton Wilder's *Our Town*, who said, looking back on her life from the land of the dead, "My, wasn't life awful … and wonderful."

… Not unlike the late Jimmy Buffet, who sang, concerning life, that some of it is magic and some of it is tragic.

… All echoes of the writer of Ecclesiastes: "There's a time to weep, and a time to laugh; a time to mourn, and a time to dance" (Eccl. 3:4).

All of which is true for most of us. For most of us, life is terrible *and* beautiful; awful *and* wonderful; filled with times to be sad *and* times to be glad.

There is a long list of ways things can go wrong in this life, and while none of us will go through all of them, all of us will go through some of them. There is a time to be sad, more than one for most of us.

For many of us, life rarely gets easy, just a different kind of hard. For every light at the end of the tunnel, there's a tunnel at the end of the light; no shortage of what the writer of Ecclesiastes called "a time to weep," not because God is that way, but because life is that way.

I cannot speak for other faith traditions, but in much of popular Christianity, we have a tendency to want to rush the weeping season. I think we fear that acknowledging the depth of our pain might somehow suggest a lapse of trust in the ultimate triumph of the promised resurrection. As a result, we tend to baptize optimism, revering upbeat positivity as though "keeping on the sunny side" is a spiritual gift.

(Across the years, I have noticed that, as a general rule, the more evangelical the church, the more talkative the funerals—as though we cannot afford to let the joy of the resurrection stand back while the pain of the loss sinks in.)

It might be more wise and true for us to let things be as tender as they are for as long as they are. When God, in 1 Samuel 16:1, asks Samuel how long Samuel is going to grieve over Saul, Samuel, as far as we know, offers no answer—perhaps because there is no answer. Grief does not come with a timeline because pain does not come with an expiration date.

Don't say "don't cry." We get to be sad about what we are sad about. There is a time to mourn, and it takes as long as it takes.

And there is a time to dance. When it's time to be sad, it's time to be sad; and when it's time to be glad, it's time to be glad.

In one of the many beautiful passages in Marilynne Robinson's *Lila*, John Ames says,

> Life on earth is difficult and grave, and marvelous. Our experience is fragmentary. Its parts don't add up…Sometimes it is hard to believe they are all parts of one thing…Joy can be joy and sorrow can be sorrow, with neither of them casting either light or shadow on the other.

Or, as the writer of Ecclesiastes said, "There is a time to weep and a time to laugh, a time to mourn and a time to dance."

And, more often than not, they merge, converge, overlap, and intersect … the time to mourn and the time to dance so inextricably entangled with one another that we sometimes find ourselves dancing on broken legs; taking the trip while taking the treatments, attending the concert in the heart of the conflict, celebrating the birth in the shadow of the death. As our late poet-priest Mary Oliver put it,

> We shake with joy, we shake with grief.
> What a time they have, these two.
> Housed as they are in the same body.

One December night many years ago, I watched a young family whose world was falling away dancing away to Brenda Lee's "Rockin' Around the Christmas Tree." It was a sacramentally human, tenderly beautiful, surgically joyful moment—a time to dance *and* a time to mourn, dancing on broken legs and laughing with broken hearts.

Which is what we do. We dance on broken legs and laugh with broken hearts because, when it's time to be glad, it's time to be glad.

For all of us, someday is going to be the last day. And, while no one can say for certain, as far as we know, we are not going to get to come back around, do this over, and get it right next time. As far as we know, this is it; the one and only life we are ever going to have. So, when it's time to be glad, it's time to be glad—even when it means dancing on broken legs.

*Though this world's full of trouble
And the path we walk is never clear,
There's a whole lot of heaven
Shining in this river of tears.*

-Iris DeMent

First Bird

As someone who rises, most days, before dawn, I have long loved to listen for the first bird heard.

I say first bird *heard* because when I asked an ornithologist, several years ago, which bird sings first each morning, they said that, because there are some birds that sing in the night, there may not actually be a first bird to sing each day—just a first bird we hear; what I call "the first bird heard."

To listen every morning for the first bird heard is, for many of us, to hear, somewhere in the background, Cat Stevens' 1972 version of Eleanor Farjeon's 1931 hymn,

> Morning has broken
> Like the first morning,
> Blackbird has spoken
> Like the first bird.

And, for some of us, each morning's first bird heard is also a small daily reminder of the way life often unfolds at the intersection of grief and relief.

In the aftermath of the worst news we have ever heard, the most crushing loss we have ever known, the hardest change we have ever endured, there is, at some point, like the first bird heard at sunrise, a first moment of rest, relief, and even joy.

When we are in the middle of the worst of life's losses, we may imagine that we will never be able to laugh again or play again; rest, sleep, or enjoy food again. But, for most of us, that day comes. As surely as there is a first bird heard each morning, there is a first meal enjoyed, a first night slept, a first laughter laughed.

Because that first time is so soon followed by the next time and all the other times, most of us can no longer remember which time was the first time we smiled again and laughed again; the first time we once again ate well and slept well; the first time we once again cared about something that doesn't matter.

… All those first times, in the middle of the worst times, when our grief was interrupted by relief, not unlike the first bird heard each morning, soon lost in the singing, winging crowd.

But, though the first bird's voice may soon be lost among the many, there is, almost every morning, that moment at the intersection of night and day when the first bird is heard; a daily sign of that beautiful sentence from Psalm 30:5, which says that weeping may last all night, but joy comes in the morning—night meeting morning, not unlike the intersection where grief meets hope.

*Hope is the thing with feathers
That perches in the soul,
And sings the tune without the words
And never stops at all.*

-Emily Dickinson

Job's Choir

"Weeping may last all night, but joy comes in the morning." With those words, the psalmist drops us off at the intersection of grief and hope. "Weeping may last all night, but joy comes in the morning;" a First Testament promise (in Ps. 30:5) that finds its Second Testament echo in those beautiful words that the writer of the gospel of John placed on the lips of Jesus: "You will have pain now. But your pain will turn to joy, and no one will take your joy from you" (John 16:22).

… A later echo of which we find in those well-known words from the 14th-century mystic Julian of Norwich: "All shall be well, all shall be well, and all manner of things shall be well" … Earlier hints of which we find in Isaiah 25:1-9 and in Revelation 5:13, Isaiah's vision of God's big feast and John's glimpse of God's great choir.

In Isaiah's vision, the whole human family is finally healed and home, seated for a banquet at the table of God.

When I was a child, folk would wonder out loud, from time to time, if we would be sad in heaven because of those who weren't there. It never occurred to us that if all were not finally, eternally healed and home, the saddest one of all would be God—God's ultimate will, the salvation of all, not only never fully done on earth, but, if any are eternally absent, also never finally done in heaven.

One imagines that if any one religion's excluding "onlyism" was to overrule and outlast God's embracing universalism, God's heart, of all hearts, would be most broken, because, according to Isaiah 25:1-9, God has already set a table and fixed a feast for the whole human family, and, apparently, is planning for every soul who ever lived to make it home in time for supper.

Job's Choir

To borrow a phrase from the wonderful song, "Crowded Table"—Brandi Carlile, Natalie Hemby, and Lori McKenna's ultimate anthem of inclusion—"God wants a house with a crowded table."

And in Isaiah's vision, that is exactly what God is going to get: God's endless table eternally crowded with the whole human family of every time and place; the whole human family, healed and home and saying grace.

Then, in Revelation 5:13, John's vision of God's eternal choir draws the circle of God's welcome even wider than Isaiah's vision of God's eternal table—God's ultimate, eventual, eternal choir, home, not only to the whole human family, but even, also, "Every creature in heaven, on earth, under the earth, and in the sea".

I cannot read those words without revisiting a vision I had about a decade ago (February 11, 2012, to be exact, according to an old daily prayer journal). I was driving alone down a street in Jackson, Mississippi, listening to the Nitty Gritty Dirt Band's version of "Will the Circle Be Unbroken?" when I found myself rolling down the window and asking, "Is it true? Is it true that somehow, someday, somewhere, some way, the circle will be unbroken?" And, from somewhere far above or deep within, in a voice as unmistakable as it was inaudible, the answer came back, "Yes. The circle will be unbroken. And it is going to be wider than anything you have ever imagined."

Needless to say, what I heard that day may have been only the echo chamber of my own desire, in which case it might mean nothing. On the other hand, it may have been the wind of the Spirit, in which case it might mean everything—and everyone.

… Everything and everyone, in a circle so unbroken and wide that it will ultimately, eventually, include, according to Revelation

5:13, not only the whole human family, but also every creature on the ground, in the sky and beneath the sea …

> aardvarks to Anglicans
> bass to Baptists
> cattle to Calvinists
> deer to Daoists
> elephants to Ebionites
> flamingos to Franciscans
> gnus to Gnostics
> hummingbirds to Hindus
> junebugs to Jesuits
> llamas to Lollards
> manatees to Methodists
> oxen to Osiandrians
> parakeets to Pentecostals
> quail to Quakers
> rhinos to Rabbis
> seals to Sikhs
> sharks to Shakers
> wildebeests to Waldensians
> yaks to Yezidis
> zebras to Zoroastrianists

… Once all the necessary confronting, judging, purging, redeeming, and reconciling has been done—no matter how long it takes—the whole human family, and all creation, singing together forever around the throne of God.

… God's choir, and Job's: all the bruised and broken ones from every tribe and tongue, people and nation, healed and home at last;

the whole human family, and all creation. Because, in the kingdom of God, all cannot be fully well for anyone until all is finally well for everyone.

Finally, and eternally, the circle will be unbroken. And all shall be well, all shall be well, all manner of things shall be well, because this is God's world, and in God's world it will be *God*, not pain or death, disease or despair, alienation or separation, guilt or shame, loss or grief, but *God* who will have the last word. And if the last word said is going to be God's, then the last thing done is going to be good.

And all the pain will turn to joy, and all the bruised-heart, bent-low souls in Job's choir will gather, at last, at the corner where grief meets hope, and sing together, each in their own language and voice, rhythm and way, "Hallelujah and Amen."

Things will not always hurt the way they do now.

-Beverly Gaventa

Epilogue

As long as we live,
God is with us.
And then, when we die,
We are with God.

www.ingramcontent.com/pod-product-compliance
Lightning Source LLC
Chambersburg PA
CBHW060220050426
42446CB00013B/3124